Snuggles with God

by Jill Roman Lord

Honor B
Tulsa, Okl

Snuggles with God
ISBN 1-56292-548-2
Copyright © 1999 by Jill Roman Lord
Published by Honor Books
P.O. Box 55388
Tulsa, Oklahoma 74155

Introduction

There is nothing like the safe, loving arms of God. He loves you and wants to be close to you. His arms are powerful and strong, but they are also gentle and loving. These rhymes and Bible verses tell about a great big God Who loves you very much! He has big dreams for you and likes to have you near Him.

Think of the times when you crawl up into your mom or dad's lap or your grandpa or grandma's lap, and snuggle up close. It feels good, doesn't it? That's because you know how much they love you. Whenever you pray or read Bible verses, you can snuggle up to God—He loves you more than anyone else does! He wants you to feel close to Him.

The words on these pages are like a great big hug from God!

To my precious blessings:

Megan

Rebecca

Jamie

and

Bill

Contents

Section 1

I'm
Special

God has made me very special;
There's no one quite like me.
He knows the things that I can do,
And all that I can be.

Be glad for all God is planning for you.
Romans 12:12

*I have so much in life to give,
There's just no room for greed.
And though I may be very young,
I still can fill a need.*

Don't hide your light! Let it shine for all.
Matthew 5:15

There's a purpose for everything,
All things under the sun.
I know God has a purpose for me,
And He has just begun!

He created everything there is—nothing
exists that he didn't make.

John 1:3

10

God wants me to be happy,
He wants me to succeed.
And if I ask, He'll give to me
Exactly what I need.

Commit your work to the Lord,
then it will succeed.

Proverbs 16:3

God has a special plan for me,
A plan that's really great.
It's better than I'd dream alone,
And I can hardly wait!

*"For I know the plans I have for you," says
the Lord, "plans for well-being and not
for trouble, to give you a future
and a hope."*
Jeremiah 29:11 NLV

12

God has buried secret treasures
Deep within my mind—
Special talents to discover
That only I can find.

∞∞∞

It is the greatness of God to keep things
hidden, but it is the greatness of kings
to find things out.

Proverbs 25:2 NLV

13

*God has given me special talents
That only I can use
To help spread joy and love around
To those who have the blues.*

*And long ages ago he planned that
we should spend these lives
in helping others.*

Ephesians 2:10

14

To find God's hidden treasures
I know that I must pray
And ask God to reveal to me
His plan, His path, His way.

And the Lord will guide you
continually, and satisfy you
with all good things.

Isaiah 58:11

15

The treasure God has planned for me
Is just for me to seek,
'Cause no one else can take my place
I'm special and unique.

In him lie hidden all the mighty,
untapped treasures of wisdom
and knowledge.

Colossians 2:3

16

I'll face some bumps along the way
When I try something new,
For that's when I will grow inside
And learn some patience, too.

Dear brothers, is your life full of difficulties
and temptations? Then be happy, for when
the way is rough, your patience has
a chance to grow.

James 1:2,3

The dreams that God will give to me
To carry out His plan
Are hard to do all by myself.
With God's help, though, I can.

I pray that you will begin to understand
how incredibly great his power is to help
those who believe him.

Ephesians 1:19

18

want to do things God's way
and be all I can be.
I know that God will show the way
And shine His light for me.

Whatever you wish will happen! And
the light of heaven will shine upon the
road ahead of you.

Job 22:28

19

I know I can do anything
If God will be my guide.
He'll help me through the ups and downs,
'Cause He is on my side.

I am sure that God who began the good work
within you will keep right on helping you
grow in his grace until his task within
you is finally finished.

Philippians 1:6

20

The Lord has blessed me with all I need
Right from my very birth.
He'll give me what I need each day
To serve Him here on earth.

And it is he who will supply all your needs
from his riches in glory.

Philippians 4:19

21

When the Lord's love is within us
He gives us special goals.
They're greater than we'd dream alone—
He knows our inner souls.

Now glory be to God who by his mighty power
at work within us is able to do far more than
we would ever dare to ask or even dream of.

Ephesians 3:20

*It doesn't matter how tall I am,
How beautiful or smart.
What counts is what God sees in me
Deep down inside my heart.*

*A man looks at the outside of a person, but
the Lord looks at the heart.*

1 Samuel 16:7 NLV

Sometimes I feel I'm not as good
As other kids my size,
But God has made me how I am—
I'm perfect in His eyes.

O God, you have declared me perfect
in your eyes.

Psalm 4:1

24

I always want things right away
It's just so hard to wait!
But God will time things perfectly
And God is never late.

*If it seems slow, do not despair, for these
things will surely come to pass. Just be patient!
They will not be overdue
a single day!*

Habukkuk 2:3

When I think I've found the path
That God wants me to go,
I know I must be patient when
I think I'm moving slow.

Slowly, steadily, surely, the time approaches
when the vision will be fulfilled.

Habukkuk 2:3

26

I'm not perfect, nobody is,
But I must try my best
To work with what God's given me.
He'll help me with the rest.

Each of us must bear some faults and
burdens of his own. For none of
us is perfect!

Galatians 6:5

When I've worked so very hard
And done the best I could,
It glorifies the Lord Himself
And makes me feel so good.

*Everyone should look at himself and see how he
does his own work. Then he can be happy in
what he has done. He should not compare
himself with his neighbor.*

Galatians 6:4 NLV

I love the Lord and know that He
Has awesome plans for me.
I'll serve Him and give praise to Him
Enthusiastically!

*Love the Lord and follow his plan for your
lives. Cling to him and serve him
enthusiastically.*

Joshua 22:5

It's nice to feel so cared about.
God's watching over me.
He knows each worry that I have
And longs to set me free!

Let him have all your worries and cares, for he
is always thinking about you and watching
everything that concerns you.

1 Peter 5:7

30

I like to smile, giggle, and laugh.
It feels good deep inside.
'Cause when I'm happy in my heart,
My joy is hard to hide.

A happy face means a glad heart.
Proverbs 15:13

God loves it when I sing to Him.
I sing and I rejoice.
He loves to hear me sing real loud
Or in a quiet voice.

I will sing and rejoice before you.
Psalm 108:1

32

The Lord loves me so very much
Just the way I am.
He made us all so different,
Just like He had planned.

God has given each of us the ability
to do certain things well.

Romans 12:6

Lots of people are everywhere
People are all about.
But I am precious to the Lord,
I know without a doubt!

How precious it is, Lord, to realize that you
are thinking about me constantly!

Psalm 139:17

34

Just knowing God is in control
Will bring me peace and rest.
It's knowing that He loves me and
Wants me to have the best!

May God our Father and the Lord Jesus
Christ give you all of his blessings, and
great peace of heart and mind.

1 Corinthians 1:3

It's great that I can learn so much.
I'm growing every day.
But let me not forget the Lord
Who made me just this way.

Don't let the excitement of being young
cause you to forget about
your Creator.

Ecclesiastes 12:1

36

The words I say reflect my heart,
My life, and attitude.
I pray my words reflect God's love
And show my gratitude.

A good man's speech reveals the rich
treasures within him.

Matthew 12:35

Section

2

Wow! God is Great!

I like when good things come my way
And everything is right.
I know God's smiling down on me
And beaming with delight.

But whatever is good and perfect
comes to us from God.

James 1:17

40

I know God loves me very much
No matter where I go.
If I'm at home or far away
His love I'll always know.

Nothing can ever separate us from his love.
Romans 8:38

41

*God promises that He'll lead me
And be my guiding light.
If I'll just put my trust in Him,
He'll help me do what's right.*

*I will instruct you (says the Lord) and guide
you along the best pathway for your life;
I will advise you and watch
your progress.*

Psalm 32:8

*I*t feels so good to be warm and loved
When I get a great big hug.
God's awesome love is all around
To keep me safe and snug.

*For we know how dearly God loves us, and we
feel this warm love everywhere within us
because God has given us the Holy Spirit
to fill our hearts with his love.*

Romans 5:5

43

Let your constant love surround me.
Hold me tightly in Your arms.
I'll feel safe and secure with You,
Away from all that harms.

Yes, Lord, let your constant love surround us,
for our hopes are in you alone.

Psalm 33:22

44

he Bible tells me many things.
The things God says, He'll do.
So, I should learn His promises,
Because they will come true.

For every promise from God shall
surely come true.

Luke 1:37

45

*We can't begin to understand
This God, to Whom we pray.
He's caring, loving, guiding, and
Perfect in every way!*

*What a God he is! How perfect in
every way!*

Psalm 18:30

46

Sometimes the road in life gets tough.
I seem to walk in place.
God will give me the strength I need
To handle what I face.

I pray that God's great power will make you
strong, and that you will have joy as you
wait and do not give up.

Colossians 1:11 NLV

The Lord will surely lead me down
The path that I should go.
If I will only seek His will
To guide me as I grow.

May he give us the desire to do his
will in everything.

1 Kings 8:58

48

$\mathcal{S}$ome things seem hard, too big for me
Like climbing a big, steep hill.
But, with God all things are possible
If it is in His will.

But with God everything is possible.
Mark 10:27

Sometimes I'm tired and burdened,
But God knows what is best.
If I will only turn to Him,
He'll give my spirit rest.

Come to me and I will give you rest . . . for I
am gentle and humble, and you shall
find rest for your souls.

Matthew 11:28,29

When I get worried, I get confused.
I turn this way and that.
But God will help it all work out,
And that's a given fact.

So don't be anxious about tomorrow. God
will take care of your tomorrow too.
Live one day at a time.

Matthew 6:34

51

Sometimes when things don't go my way,
And I'm the one to blame,
When I've been acting less than good,
God loves me just the same.

How kind he is! How good he is!
So merciful, this God of ours!
Psalm 116:5

52

I can't do all things by myself,
But if I'll only ask,
God will give me courage and strength
To carry out the task.

The Lord makes us strong!
Psalm 81:1

53

I'll give my problems to the Lord,
They're much too big to carry.
He will always help me out
When things get hard or scary.

Give your burdens to the Lord.
He will carry them.
Psalm 55:22

54

I know God will never leave me
No matter what I face.
No problem is too big for God.
He'll gladly show His grace.

Those who know Your name will put
their trust in You. For You, O Lord, have
never left alone those
who look for You.
Psalm 9:10 NLV

55

It feels good to be loved so much
No matter what I do.
If I mess up, God just forgives
And He still loves me too.

∞∞∞

And to experience this love for yourselves,
though it is so great that you will never see
the end of it or fully know
or understand it.

Ephesians 3:19

When I cry and when I feel sad
Or need a gentle touch,
It helps to know I'm special and
God loves me very much.

Yet there is one ray of hope:
his compassion never ends.

Lamentations 3:21

God is everywhere around me
Although I may not see,
He's right here when I ask for Him
Wherever I may be.

You will look for Me and find Me,
when you look for Me with
all your heart.

Jeremiah 29:13 NLV

Tiny birds don't seem to worry
About their food or clothes.
God surely cares for me—
He loves me more than those!

You are more important than
many small birds.
Matthew 10:31 NLV

When I am scared and want to hide
Someplace I'd feel secure,
The Lord wants me to turn to Him.
He'll comfort me, for sure.

You are my hiding place from
every storm of life.

Psalm 32:7

God works in mysterious ways,
All things just seem to flow.
How He makes things work out so well
I think I'll never know.

Then you will learn from your own
experience how his ways will
really satisfy you.

Romans 12:2

God shows us His almighty works
Each and every day.
So, I must stop and notice them
And look along the way.

Oh, what a wonderful God we have!
Romans 11:33

God loves His children very much,
And this He wants made known.
The Lord is like a dad to us
He calls us all His own.

See how very much our heavenly Father
loves us, for he allows us to be
called his children.

1 John 3:1

63

There's so much, Lord, to think about
There's so much that's unknown:
The mighty miracles You work,
The splendor of You alone.

I will meditate about your glory, splendor,
majesty and miracles.

Psalm 145:5

64

I know that I will never know
A love so deep and wide
As the love God has for me—
A love He'll never hide.

And may you be able to feel and understand,
as all God's children should, how long, how
wide, how deep, and how high
his love really is.
Ephesians 3:18

65

Section 3

Our God is a wonderful Friend,
Great blessings He will send.
He loves us more than we can know.
He's with us 'til the end.

For this great God is our God
forever and ever.
Psalm 48:14

here are many things that I can learn
From Father up above.
The first that I must pass along
is His greatest gift of love.

∞∞∞

There are three things that remain—faith,
hope, and love—and the greatest
of these is love.

1 Corinthians 13:13

Love is very patient and kind,
Love tries to understand.
Love sees the best in others, and
Love lends a helping hand.

Love is very patient and kind.
1 Corinthians 13:4

*I love God, yes, I really do,
And He wants me to know
That when I love all those around,
My love for Him will show.*

If you love God, love your brother also.
1 John 4:21 NLV

71

I'm in this world to share God's love
With others all around,
And when I learn to pass it on
A new joy will be found.

And may the Lord make your love to
grow and overflow to each other
and everyone else.

1 Thessalonians 3:12

72

I'll spread God's love to everyone,
And then, I'm sure I'll find
It feels good in my heart to love
And feels good to be kind.

And whatever you do, do it with
kindness and love.

1 Corinthians 16:14

73

When I help someone I don't know,
The angels find delight.
The heavens smile down on me,
Because I've done what's right.

Don't forget to be kind to strangers, for
some who have done this have entertained
angels without realizing it!

Hebrews 13:2

74

I know God loves me very much
And that's an awful lot.
He wants me to love just like Him
And give it all I've got.

Love each other just as much
as I love you.
John 13:34

The more I love, the more I serve—
The two go hand in hand.
The more I serve, the more I receive.
Try it! You'll understand.

It is more blessed to give than to receive.
Acts 20:35

When I help others, they will see
It's love that really counts.
I'll find that love comes back to me
In great big huge amounts!

Your gift will return to you in full and
overflowing measure, pressed down, shaken
together to make room for more,
and running over.
Luke 6:38

77

*G*od shows how love can really spread,
*A*nd this I do believe.
The more that I help others, then
The more I will receive.

*The way you give to others is the way you
will receive in return.*

Luke 6:38 NLV

78

When I love the Lord above
This love just spreads, I learn.
It makes me want to help and serve
And brings joy in return.

I myself have gained much joy and comfort
from your love, my brother, because your
kindness has so often refreshed the
hearts of God's people.
Philemon 1:7

79

It's good to love my mom and dad
My sisters and my brothers,
And God wants me to also share
This same love with all others.

Love each other with brotherly affection.
Romans 12:10

God believes I can truly love—
It must come from my heart.
If I can love and show I care,
Then I will do my part.

Don't just pretend that you love others:
really love them.

Romans 12:9

To laugh and talk and play with us,
To help a little more,
To love us when we're not so nice,
That's what God made friends for.

A friend loves at all times.
Proverbs 17:17 NLV

I'll always stand right by my friends
No matter what it takes,
Because friends forgive each other
And love forgets mistakes.

Love forgets mistakes.
Proverbs 17:9

Love each other in work and play
To glorify His name.
Loving each other no matter what
Should be our daily aim.

Let love be your greatest aim.
1 Corinthians 14:1

When others are not nice to me,
Lord, help me to be strong.
Help me to love them anyway,
'Cause being mean is wrong.

He will give you the strength to endure.
2 Corinthians 1:7

85

*I know that I'm not perfect,
I sometimes make mistakes.
But I still try to love and care,
And that is what it takes.*

Most important of all, continue to show deep love for each other, for love makes up for many of your faults.

1 Peter 4:8

If someone hurts you, turn away,
'Cause hurting back is wrong.
We should be kind to everyone
And try to get along.

Do not let anyone pay back for the bad he
received. But look for ways to do good to
each other and to all people.

1 Thessalonians 5:15 NLV

*O*h, think of what this world could be
If everyone would love.
We all would be so full of joy—
We'd please the Lord above.

*Then make me truly happy by loving each
other and agreeing wholeheartedly with
each other, working together with one
heart and mind and purpose.*

Philippians 2:2

*G*od showed how much He loves us all
By sending us His Son.
No matter what our race or creed,
We must love everyone.

*A*nd you must love your neighbor just as
much as you love yourself.
Luke 10:27

89

Jesus says to love each other.
So that's what I will do.
Jesus says, "Love one another
As much as I love you."

Love each other as much as I love you.
John 15:12

I want my love to overflow
Like Jesus' love for me.
If everyone would love that much,
Then we'd live happily.

Live with love as Christ loved you.
Ephesians 5:2 NLV

It's good to say, "I'm sorry"
For things that I've done wrong.
It shows my friends I really care
And keeps our friendship strong.

A gentle answer turns away anger, but a
sharp word causes anger.

Proverbs 15:1 NLV

92

Lord, help me to love everyone
Although it may be tough.
It's easy to love just my friends,
But that is not enough.

Love your enemies!
Luke 6:35

If I see a friend who's all alone
And standing far away,
Help me, Lord, to take her hand
So she will come and play.

Never abandon a friend.
Proverbs 27:10

God wants us all to love and share
And really get along.
It's fun to play together and,
This love will keep us strong.

∞∞

Live in peace with each other.

Romans 12:16 NLV

Section 4

Dear God . . .

Jesus taught us many things.
He taught us how to pray.
The Lord's Prayer is a special prayer
To guide our prayers each day.

And now about prayer . . . Pray
along these lines.
Matthew 6:5,9

Lord, You're majestic and holy,
You love us all the same.
We praise You and respect You, and
Honor Your Holy Name.

Our Father in heaven, we honor
your holy name.

Matthew 6:9

I know You have a perfect plan
For all things on this earth.
I pray You'll lead me down the path
That You've planned since my birth.

We ask that your kingdom will come now.
May your will be done here on earth, just
as it is in heaven.

Matthew 6:10

100

he birds don't know what they will eat,
But all the birds You feed.
We trust that You will also provide
The food our bodies need.

Give us our food again today, as usual.
Matthew 6:11

101

Friends, we must forgive each other,
Christ told us when He came.
God forgives us when we sin,
So, we must do the same.

And forgive us our sins, just as we have
forgiven those who have sinned
against us.

Matthew 6:12

I know there will be temptations
To do what may be wrong.
I ask for God's help in these times,
That He will keep me strong.

*Don't bring us into temptation, but deliver
us from the Evil One. Amen.*

Matthew 6:13

103

When I wake up in the morning,
I say a little prayer.
God likes it when I talk with Him
In bed or anywhere.

You must pray at all times as the Holy
Spirit leads you to pray.
Ephesians 6:18 NLV

Sometimes I like to sit alone
When everything is still.
I like to think and talk to God
And ask Him for His will.

And when you draw close to God,
God will draw close to you.

James 4:8

God wants us to pray for others.
We should go to any length
To lift their problems up to God,
So He will give them strength.

We are praying, too, that you will be filled
with his mighty, glorious strength so that
you can keep going no matter
what happens.
Colossians 1:11

106

When I see someone hurting,
I'll keep them in my prayers.
So God will love and comfort them
And show how much He cares.

Is anyone among you suffering? He
should keep on praying about it.

James 5:13

There's lots to pray for every day
For those who are in need.
For relatives and friends of mine,
It's good to pray, indeed.

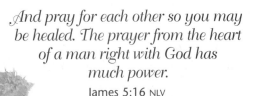

And pray for each other so you may
be healed. The prayer from the heart
of a man right with God has
much power.

James 5:16 NLV

I'll think of others all around
When I'm on bended knee.
I'll say a little prayer for them
And know God hears my plea.

Pray much for others; plead for God's mercy
upon them; give thanks for all he is going
to do for them.

1 Timothy 2:1

It's so easy to be joyful
When things just go my way.
But I must pray, give thanks with joy
On every single day!

Always be joyful. Always
keep on praying.
1 Thessalonians 5:16,17

110

When we ask God for anything,
We must not ask in greed.
We know He hears us, and we trust
He'll give us what we need.

*And we are sure of this, that he will listen
to us whenever we ask him for anything
in line with his will.*

1 John 5:14

111

I can ask God for anything.
And if I do believe,
If it's His will, then it will be.
His blessings I'll receive.

You can get anything—anything you ask
for in prayer—if you believe.

Matthew 21:22

$\mathcal{S}$ometimes I just get so confused,
I don't know what to do.
I need to pray about it and
Know Christ will help me through.

*And now just as you trusted Christ to
save you, trust him, too, for
each day's problems.*

Colossians 2:6

113

Some things just seem impossible,
No matter how hard I try.
I can turn and ask God to help,
And He will get me by.

But with God, everything is possible.
Matthew 19:26

114

Help me to pray for everything—
All thoughts that cross my mind.
If I'm worried, I'll turn to God.
His comfort I will find.

Don't worry about anything; instead,
pray about everything.
Philippians 4:6

I know that God will always help,
If only I will ask.
I need to ask and seek His will.
That's such a simple task.

Ask, and you will be given what you ask for.
Seek, and you will find. Knock, and the
door will be opened.

Matthew 7:7

116

The Lord will grant us peace and rest
Each and every day.
Whenever I start to worry,
Dear Jesus, help me pray.

*Don't worry about anything; instead, pray about
everything . . . If you do this you will experience
God's peace, which is far more wonderful than
the human mind can understand.*

Philippians 4:6,7

117

When I have problems and life is tough,
Or things won't go my way,
I know that God will help me if
I'll only stop and pray.

Be patient in trouble, and
prayerful always.
Romans 12:12

118

I've prayed to God and asked for help,
But now it's getting late.
I trust that He will answer me.
He may be saying, "Wait!"

∞∞∞

The Lord is wonderfully good to those
who wait for him, to those
who seek for him.

Lamentations 3:25

119

Dear Lord, please reveal to me
Parts of me that are weak.
I want to serve You better each day.
Improvements I will seek.

Search me, O God, and know my heart; test my
thoughts. Point out anything you find in me that
makes you sad, and lead me along the
path of everlasting life.

Psalm 139:23,24

120

Lord, I know You hear my prayers,
And answers always come.
You know exactly what I need.
You'll give me that—plus some.

When I pray, you answer me, and
encourage me by giving me the
strength I need.

Psalm 138:3

121

Oh Lord, You know what's in my heart.
You know when I am sad.
You hear my prayers and answer them
And want me to be glad.

*I love the Lord because he hears my
prayers and answers them.*

Psalm 116:1

The Lord, He always seems to know
Just what I need each day.
He'll send whatever is best for me,
If I'll just stop and pray.

And if we really know he is listening when
we talk to him and make our requests,
then we can be sure that he
will answer us.
1 John 5:15

*When I pray I must be sure
My prayer comes from my heart.
I must be honest and sincere
Before I even start.*

*Don't recite the same prayer over and
over. . . . Remember, your Father knows
exactly what you need even
before you ask him!*
Matthew 6:7,8

124

It is good to pray together.
It is good to pray alone.
However you feel comfortable
To make your wishes known.

But when you pray, go away by yourself, all
alone, and shut the door behind you and pray to
your Father secretly, and your Father, who
knows your secrets, will reward you.

Matthew 6:6

125

God wants to know what's on my mind.
He likes it when I pray.
It's fun to watch Him answer prayers
In His own perfect way.

Tell God your needs and don't forget
to thank him for his answers.

Philippians 4:6

126

*I know I'm just a little child,
But God still hears my prayer.
He's not too busy to listen.
He's promised to be there.*

*He will answer the prayer of those
in need. He will not turn from
their prayer.*

Psalm 102:17 NLV

127

Section 5

Thank You,
Lord

*Jesus was kind and gentle
to everyone He knew
and kept a thankful heart
and in God's love He grew.*

*My prayer for all of them is that they
will be of one heart and mind, just
as you and I are, Father.*

John 17:21

130

It is nice to give thanks to the Lord
For all that He has done.
He's given me so many blessings—
And He has just begun!

For the Lord is great, and should be
highly praised.
1 Chronicles 16:25

I'll give thanks in the morning
When I get out of bed.
It gives me strength and also puts
Good thoughts up in my head.

Every morning tell him, "Thank you for your
kindness," and every evening rejoice in
all his faithfulness.

Psalm 92:2

It's always nice to give God thanks
For all that He has done.
He sends me blessings every day
In rain and snow and sun.

May he grant you your heart's desire and
fulfill all your plans.

Psalm 20:4

There's so much to be thankful for
From God Who is adored.
So I must give thanks through His Son,
Jesus Christ, our Lord.

Always give thanks for everything to
our God and Father in the name
of our Lord Jesus Christ.

Ephesians 5:20

I wake up in the morning, and
I jump right out of bed.
I thank the Lord for giving me
This day that lies ahead.

*This is the day the Lord has made. We
will rejoice and be glad in it.*

Psalm 118:24

*G*ive thanks to God in the morning
*F*or the beauty of the day,
*F*or all the wonders it will bring,
*F*or good to come my way.

I will sing about your lovingkindness
and your justice, Lord. I will
sing your praises!

Psalm 101:1

136

*Think of all God's given to you
And thank Him in return.
Whether your list is big or small,
Your blessings you will learn.*

How refreshed I am by your blessings!
Psalm 92:10

137

God's favorite kinds of prayers
Are those that give Him praise.
I will lift up my thanks to Him
And praise Him all my days.

Praise the Lord, who does these
miracles for you.
Joel 2:26

Shout with joy and celebrate!
The Lord God loves us so!
Shout with joy and give Him thanks
His blessings overflow!

Shout with joy before the Lord, O earth!
Psalm 100:1

139

I praise God in the morning,
I praise God in the night,
I praise God in the afternoon,
In darkness and in light.

O God, my heart is quiet and confident. No
wonder I can sing your praises!

Psalm 57:7

140

$\mathcal{P}$raise is a way of thanking God
For His almighty ways.
To express our love and awe for Him,
We give Him thanks and praise!

O Lord, I will praise you with all my heart,
and tell everyone about the marvelous
things you do.

Psalm 9:1

141

Give thanks to God and shout with joy
Oh, dance and jump and sing!
God loves to see the happiness
That giving thanks can bring!

∞∞∞

Sing to the Lord, all the earth! Sing of his
glorious name! Tell the world how
wonderful he is.

Psalm 66:1,2

Because I know He listens to me
I will keep on saying
All my thanks and praise to Him, and
I will keep on praying.

Because he bends down and listens, I will
pray as long as I breathe!

Psalm 116:2

143

We children do the best we can
To give the Lord our praise.
We sing our songs and say our prayers.
He loves our precious ways.

You have taught the little children to
praise you perfectly.

Psalm 8:2

144

Help me to have a thankful heart
Though troubles come my way.
I know that those will help me grow
And trust the Lord each day.

And always be thankful.
Colossians 3:15

145

I'm thankful for the good times, Lord,
When things just seem to flow.
In tougher times, I'll give thanks, too.
These times will help me grow.

*No matter what happens, always be thankful,
for this is God's will for you who
belong to Christ Jesus.*

1 Thessalonians 5:18

146

So many good things come my way
Though I have hard times too.
I'm thankful in the ups and downs,
'Cause Jesus helps me through.

Come to me and I will give you rest . . . for
I give you only light burdens.
Matthew 11:28,30

147

Dear God, thank You for the sparrows
That fly so high and free.
You give them food and so I know
That You'll take care of me.

*Look at the birds! They don't worry about what to
eat—they don't need to sow or reap or store up food—for
your heavenly Father feeds them. And you are far
more valuable to him than they are.*

Matthew 6:26

148

Thank You, Lord, for loving me,
Even when I sin.
There's so much I can thank You for.
Where do I begin?

Think about all you can praise God for
and be glad about.

Philippians 4:8

149

Thank You, Lord, for all Your gifts,
For everything that's good.
For giving me the things I need,
Just like You said You would.

He fills my life with good things!
Psalm 103:5

150

Thank You, Lord, for giving me
Two roads that I could take.
I can choose either right or wrong.
Choose right, for heaven's sake!

Turn from all known sin and spend your
time in doing good. Try to live in peace
with everyone; work hard at it.

Psalm 34:14

151

Thank You, Lord, for loving me
And holding me so tight.
Thank You for forgiving me
And teaching me what's right.

My thanks will be his praise.
Psalm 69:30

I'm thankful that God sent Jesus
And for His saving grace,
For loving me through my mistakes,
And for His warm embrace.

Hold tightly to the pattern of truth I taught
you, especially concerning the faith and
love Christ Jesus offers you.

2 Timothy 1:13

153

Dear God, thank You for loving me,
Imperfect and with flaws,
For sending Christ to be our Friend,
And teaching us Your laws.

God's purpose in this was that we
should praise God and give glory to him
for doing these mighty
things for us.
Ephesians 1:12

Thank You, Lord, for my family,
For all the friends I meet,
For trees to climb, and things to learn.
Your love just can't be beat!

It is good to say, "Thank you"
to the Lord.

Psalm 92:1

155

Your blessings fill my life, oh Lord.
You've loved me from the start.
You've given me so many things.
I thank You from my heart.

Lord, with all my heart I thank you.

Psalm 138:1

*O*h, give thanks to the mighty Lord!
His goodness will not end.
His loving kindness never stops;
His love for us won't bend.

∽∾∽

Oh, give thanks to the Lord, for he is
good; his lovingkindness
continues forever.

Psalms 136:1

About the Author

Jill Roman Lord is a Nurse Anesthetist (CRNA) at Carolinas Medical Center in Charlotte, North Carolina. She and her family attend the University City United Methodist Church where she directs the preschool choir and teaches toddler Sunday School. She is also active in family retreat and Disciples Bible Study program. Jill seeks to enrich children's  lives by illuminating the Lord's gracious love and mercy. She lives with her husband and three children in Charlotte, North Carolina.

Additional copies of this book and other titles by Honor Books
are available from your local bookstore.

God's Little Instruction Book for Kids
God's Little Instruction Book 2 for Kids
The Candymaker's Gift
The Living Nativity
WWJD for Kids

If you have enjoyed this book, or if it has
impacted your life, we would like to hear from you.
Please contact us at:

Honor Books
Department E
P.O. Box 55388
Tulsa, Oklahoma 74155
Or by e-mail at info@honorbooks.com